THE COLOR SHE GAVE GRAVITY

STEPHANIE HEIT

the operating system print//document

THE COLOR SHE GAVE GRAVITY

ISBN 978-1-946031-02-0 | Library of Congress Control Number 2016962664
copyright © 2017 by Stephanie Heit; this edition © 2020
designed and edited by Elæ Lynne DeSilva-Johnson

is released under a Creative Commons CC-BY-NC-ND (Attribution, Non Commercial, No Derivatives
License: its reproduction is encouraged for those who otherwise could not afford its purchase in the
case of academic, personal, and other creative usage from which no profit will accrue.
Complete rules and restrictions are available at: http://creativecommons.org/licenses/by-nc-nd/3.0/
For additional questions regarding reproduction, quotation, or to request a pdf for review
contact operator@theoperatingsystem.org

cover photos © Gwynneth VanLaven: front, "Crossing Visible"; back, "Asphalta angelica"

Image Description Front: Black with orange traffic cone positioned in double yellow lines of street.
Progression of a body across the space, yellow-green blur above multiple lower legs.
Image Description Back: Hand reaches out from yellow-green diaphanous sleeve to touch asphalt.

This text was set in Athelas, Helvetica Neue, Minion Pro, OCR A Standard, and Franchise.
Operating System books in limited edition and small run are printed and bound by Spencer Printing, in
Honesdale, PA, in the USA, with distribution to the trade and POD via Ingram.

As of 2020 all of our titles are available for donation-only download via our Open Access Library:
http://www.theoperatingsystem.org/os-open-access-community-publications-library/

the operating system//press
141 Spencer Street #203
Brooklyn, NY 11205
www.theoperatingsystem.org

THE COLOR SHE GAVE GRAVITY

ADVANCE PRAISE for 'THE COLOR SHE GAVE GRAVITY'

"[I]n the slow gestures/of a person adjusting/to too much light" and with the faith of a chemist, Stephanie Heit sets fire inside her own dark and offers "light someone not yet arrived/ will understand." The Color She Gave Gravity is a breathtaking (which is to say, life-giving) book that both stills and energizes by breaking and reforming the unseen bonds of DNA, language, geography, and history." - TC Tolbert

"Stephanie Heit's The Color She Gave Gravity is a sonorous force field calling on tenderness, care, vigilance and abandon. An all-encompassing clarity saturates mind, spirit, movement and emotion. To locate the blind spot and unburden experience of the horizon's relentless pressure—this is what the text does tenfold, imparting and dispelling the inexplicable along peripheries and in intimately centered frames of movement: gorgeously evocative and intensely realized capacious psychic flows." - Brenda Iijima

"Stephanie Heit has choreographed, in her first full-length poetry collection, a deeply engaging articulation of the interplay between mental illness and the creative instinct, history and destiny, and limitation and willful boundary. Here, we have an author brave enough to say "I suffer" and talented enough to excavate the lyrical beauty of that suffering. The Color She Gave Gravity offers the reader a textured view of a graceful body torn between trying to remember and trying to forget." - Airea D. Matthews

"In these fierce, moving poems, we witness a self as it seeks its right path through those landscapes we call world. We are taken along, wandering through urban streets or across beaches that once were lakes, sometimes dreamily, sometimes searingly awake, digging through stories and years. These poems enact one of our most potent human gifts: our ability to find ourselves — tumbling, falling down, standing up — in proprioceptive relation to everything in our earthly realm." - Eleni Sikelianos

for Petra
who makes it beautiful

Penumbra	13
Z Cycle	35
Lake Etymology	53
Enter Amnesiac	69
Quiet Anatomy	85
Coda	103
Open Loop Triptych	105
She Had Windows for Organs	108
Notes and Commentary	109

A book is an elegant technique for folding a lot of surface area into a compact, convenient volume; a library is likewise a compounding of such volumes, a temple of compression of many worlds.

REBECCA SOLNIT

The most precious things will become silence and water.

NICOLE BROSSARD

PENUMBRA

the city stands

out the window

dreaming a night

with no voices

X's on a map

made of water

islands of skin

we reach the place hands die from too little touch

we help each other

down the train steps

into the city we shape

in the slow gestures

of a person adjusting

to too much light

the roads are breath sounds

we talk in errant time signatures

she unloosens her hair

shortens the distance

between where we are going

she visions Belgrade

blueprint for a peninsula

I have a ticket for something we forgot

city halflit & tired on a Friday

it is always Friday

we wear black to mourn

the other week days

streetlights   numbered houses

dresses build themselves into turrets

we make silences except

I remember the ease of bodies before words

we wait for the next station

bedrock   agate   broken mirrors

dresses soiled with afternoon fog

she creates keyholes for doors that lead

outside to inside

I trace where blue would be had we thought *sky*

an alley out of fingers

we balance

our feet

scavengers

trained against memory

we lie across the page

a collection of days

on a map mostly blue

the city stands over water

we take the long way

she thinks

vibration   gateway   compass

the possibility of losing

her mind

wanders backwards

she leaves

her luggage at the station

hands free pendulums

shuttle her

to junctures she forgets

to relax

stumbles

she unbuckles

her shoes

wades into night waves

white dress

a halo around

her distant figure

going deeper

I hold the afternoon

white knuckled she

slips the dress

over geography

travelled by the careful

arrangement of water bottles

nightgown echo doorknob sister

I no longer find her with words

the sound of bells

erosion of consonants

city without tears

water exiled from water

riverine the city breathes

wrought iron lungs

a cradle of mortar & rib

we don't need architecture

the city temporary

glass   rock   & metatarsal

always   *the sea*

your hand

some kind of red

she sleeps in tourist office maps

latitude imprints face

the morning

she asks the color

we gave gravity

she crosses the street

to get us coffee

I hold my breath

trusting acceleration

she never looks both ways

be careful to make only curved lines

coin toss decides

our precise movement

together or apart

fearful of trespass

I lock the doors

to keep her

from falling

the light turns to face us

her reflection disappears

from the second floor window

she can't open

darkness with all this sun

render smooth these sharp thoughts

we retrace history

against a wall tilted

you are making all this up

back & forth

in search of

the city before

at the end of the train line

the one we brought luggage to

assembly of tracks

bent to our feet

do bodies create a city?

I feel her

trapped in

the city after

zip code washed

drunken by tides

rose petals   birdsong

the bodies we touch for arrival

ghosts

the line torn from my notebook

we enter backs to the outside

disappeared

I send her a confidential message

where are you?

the city moves into the sea

quicksand   shell   invertebrate

soft insides of buildings lose foundation

yellow ball   dry erase board   static

she forgets the sequence

stands center

on the line

weight shifts

until she appears

my hair is longer than you think

the city shuts down

bags packed with folded

architecture asphalt greenspace

silhouette light turned off

feather & sand brushed from our eyes

we toss the atlas

ink fading

into ocean

Chopin ends the day in e minor

lines collapse

ceilings give weight to floors

we push the sky

with our spines

wish between vertebrae

a city less broken

where streetlights glow

instead of this dark mistaken for night

here stars deliver messages

a thousand years overdue

we breathe out the windows

light someone not yet arrived

will understand

she flexes her foot & places it at an angle

to my circular wrist motions

the dresses off white

whispers escape the seams

I don't know which voice is yours

we get smaller as the sun rises

when the line curves past seeing

there will be no more Fridays

on a byway we walk diagonally

through barbed wire

the city speaks

in perfect unison

the way people fade

Z CYCLE

Once upon a time you watch the night. Adrenalin ready for the darkness in spite of overlapped curtains, shut closets, ritual goodnight conversation. You stare it down. Listen for the creaks the cries of dark: hyperaware, shallow breathed, five-year-old body taut. You fall asleep from sheer exhaustion when you aren't looking. Before the dark was inside you. Before the creaks the cries of dark came out your mouth. Before night took root in your brain and spread like electricity multitudinous, genomic, internet codes coding neural pathways rocking out to suffering as you try to find an exit an entrance the button to push the cord to pull. Past too far past retrieval into some kind of Dante Inferno type purgatory level. You've eaten too many pomegranate seeds destined to sleep or not sleep with hell every night.

16 hour somnolent reprieve mimicks death. Weight of bones heavy with fat, muscle, skin. Animal in hibernation you burrow between lids of covers. Curtain closes. Solid stillness. Deeper than dream. Unconscious pool of raw. Wake more tired than when you went to sleep. Push the covers away and feel the room air. Roll slowly to your side to sit on the bed's edge. Horizontal to vertical. Blood recirculates. The day inches below your feet. Stand and enter. You do it in your head. Give up and sleep more. Try again. Two dimensional line that takes the will of the Rockies, Lake Michigan, 9+Chilean earthquake to realize yourself 3D and human. Morning becomes afternoon. Sun's shadows across the walls skylight and warning.

Donkey, cat and horse. Backward by seven's. List of words: *key diary railroad yellow lipstick.* Connect the numbers. Draw a triangle. Recite: *key diary railroad yellow lipstick.* Change into the gown. Remove jewelry, your watch. Hand these to your dad for safe-keeping. Get on the bed. Down the elevator to the Post Anesthesia Care Unit. IV. Wait your turn. Beeping machines. Cramped room. *How was breakfast?* Anesthesiologist humor. Recite name and birthdate. *Toredol, flumazenil, propofol, succinylcholine.* See the whooshing sound behind your eyes. You don't dream. You don't remember the seizure. Some part of you wakes up in recovery to answer orientation questions. Upstairs you don't know what time it is or the location of your watch. Dress and wheelchair it to the cafeteria for lunch. Sleep the four hour drive home. Dinner. Sleep 14 hour night. Repeat 3x/week then 2 then 1 then every other week then repeat and reset. You fall in love with the anesthesia. Ask the doctors to add a little more off the record.

Chelated magnesium. Valerian that smells like feet. Spikenard on the forehead and soles. Watch the ceiling as if it were Sunday night *Downton Abbey*. Don't notate the time and how many hours until you have to get up. Witness the night. The 4 am train thundering by horns directed at people who instead of trying to sleep wander the tracks counting boards instead of sheep. You don't count anything. Have tried meditation, warm baths, no TV or stimulation and still this duet with awake won't let you off the dance floor but keeps you spinning until dawn when the birds start announcing a new day as if you care the earth rotated its axis while the sun stayed put you rode the ceiling white but close study variances of color from bad paint jobs the interface where wall meets ceiling a ridge of build-up then the color in the backs of your eyelids as you try and try not to try.

Imagine an island, waves, rum drink with mint garnish, saltwater smell, luminous sun and all that other beach crap. Safe and relaxed your cares piled on the floor like the clothes you haven't hung up and the dishes in the sink with chopped tomatoes stuck on the cutting board. Your alarm rings. Curse its violent sound. Slam down the snooze. Sleep once again eluded you. Ocean waves took you under where no oxygen left you gasping. Relax. Tuck those covers chin side tight. There is always tonight. Another chance to woo those nomad Z's. Make them yours.

Take 2 mg of *ativan*. Watch fireflies and contemplate a regular humid summer night where the paperbacks all fold open. Buzz of other people's air conditioners an orchestra. Those fuckers with their AC and closed windows while you have sweaty armpits and crotch. Walk the two blocks to the 24 hour Kroger. Buy Reese's king size peanut butter cups knowing you won't save the other two for later like you're promising yourself. At home watch sleep from a distance, that whore you'd like to bed who lies with everyone but you.

3 am on the dot. Every night. Count the hours since you went to bed and be grateful for those. Know how it is going to go but you, idiot optimist, think it could be different. Pee but don't flush to not disturb the night silence. Let the water run warm over your hands. Return to bed as if it is no big deal. Pull the covers up over your shoulders and curl fetal style on your right side. Wait. Wait some more. Your mother's voice: *at least you are resting.* Stay in the same position afraid to disrupt that film of nothingness advancing on you unexpectedly so you won't be able to pinpoint when it happened but say, *I guess I fell asleep.* You want to be the girl who says that. Want those words in your mouth so badly you can taste them. Drool puddling out your lips, mucous caked on your eyes, so deep you don't hear the Monday morning garbage truck don't see the seductive light job of dawn. So delighted you want to fuck the Greek god of sleep whose name you don't remember but it would be good to fuck in a bed to do something in it besides sleep or not sleep.

The guides say don't read in bed, don't talk on the phone, don't have any association with bed besides sleep. You want to hunt down the people who have written those guides. People who are sleeping tidily in their self satisfaction that they have made the world a better place with their glossy brochures endorsed by the *Sleep Disorders Association of America*. You hope they have nightmares, messed up REM cycles, and you want to go on but are too tired to be angry too tired to think of anything besides how tired you are. You think about how death would feel like sleep and begin to tumble the idea around like the clothes cascading in the dryer at the Stadium Laundromat so at least you can try to sleep in clean pajamas, clean sheets. One of the guides probably recommends clean linens perhaps lavender infused dryer sheets.

Go to therapy. Talk about the reasons you may have trouble falling asleep. How sleep is a separation a letting go. How not sleeping could be a defense against feeling. Reply you have always been an expert sleeper. Insomnia is a side effect of meds and not the other psychological bullshit applied like a panacea to your whole life. Next dance for two hours. Return home after buying sweet cherries at the farmers market. Eat a bunch until you picture your insides that addictive red past red of cherry flesh. Lay down on the couch to rest your eyes. Move to the bed to rest them further. Don't take your contacts out because this is only a 30 minute nap if you're lucky. Sleep. Don't fall. Plunge. Into the ripe underbelly of fatigue famished and violent finally subdued by an Olympic sleep warranting a gold. Continue 1 hour 2 hours at 3 wake up for a moment, note the 80 degree afternoon, sun coming through the window, flower bouquet on nightstand, sweat soaked clothes and roll over to sleep some more. Marathon Sleeper, push the edge of nap until afternoon blurs to night. Your brain sings. Neurotransmitter and receptor fires stoked and ready to roar. Body hums. Bard-like belt out an ode to the hope-to-hell-to-be-repeated-soon wonder of that miraculous state of *o wherefore art thou* sleep.

Holy like communion or a fix. *Ambien* small white pill. Shake the bottle like castanets like salsa dancing with a partner who is too good to let go. When you can't sleep take more to override any tolerance. Addiction warning label on the side of the bottle. The convict feel when the CVS pharmacist asks for your driver's license. 2 months later. 3 months. 4. You still need it. Have tried going without and wide awake watched the entire night. Weigh risks vs. benefits. Sleep deprived vs. possible addiction. A decade ago you lied to a walk-in clinic doctor about invented insomnia to get a scrip. To kick it all down the hatch sweet suicide you didn't have the guts to do. Now you take them one at a time. Relief when the bottle is full. Rainy day guarantee that makes sleep a better companion. Relax knowing if it gets bad enough you are prepared. One foot in front of the other a tightrope no one sees.

Tired of listening to their stories. Your story. Having people say they understand. The 356 suggestions this week alone from well-meaning-do-gooders. You get on a soapbox with an old school dark blue megaphone and projectile lecture: *raw food, chelation therapy, kundalini mantras, rescue remedy, haircut, buy a dress, half smile, gratitude journal, article on jogging as best medicine for treatment resistant depression, emotional freedom techniques, gluten free diet, Jesus, Buddha, Mother Earth, Hitachi 250R, Freudian analysis, Jungian analysis, jatamansi oil, biomagnetismo, 5HTP...+336* other suggestions are not going to save them. But what has happened to you won't happen to them because they will: *rawfoodchelation therapykundalinimantrasrescueremedyhaircutbuyadresshalfsmile gratitudejournalarticleonjoggingasbestmedicinefortreatmentresistant depressionemotionalfreedomtechniquesglutenfreedietJesusBuddha MotherEarthHitachi250RFreudiananalysisJungiananalysis jatamansioilbiomagnetismo5HTP...+336* others instead of be with you, hold your hand and shut the fuck up. Tired from ranting you put the dark blue megaphone down, step off the soap box knowing they didn't hear you, that you'll hear the same 356 suggestions next week and you are tired and start crying because you are tired and because you've tried all 356 suggestions and you still hurt.

Enter the day. Covers tossed aside to move horizontal to vertical and greet the newly awakened tribe you've grown to hate. Their fresh start wake up stretch coffee smell Folger's morning way. The way you never feel. You look in the mirror requisite dark circles, annoying acne on neck and scalp from meds. Try on a smile that sags and goes neutral. *Plum Dandy*. The name of the MAC lipstick you used to wear when you used to wear lipstick. *Tired but wired*. A thin wakefulness tinged with the refrigerator buzz and the fan that goes on in the laptop when it gets too hot.

The term all-nighter becomes all-weeker. Death by exhaustion. How that would look. How you'd wear tiredness past season, vintage. Like sleep will never happen again. Like falling in love when you're not. Complexity of moments synchronized in two lives to create a meeting. Sleep, an indifferent lover, keeps its own schedule. You brush shoulders at sunrise when it exits and you join the awake world except you aren't stretching and shaking off dream's lovely web but racking hours in your personal sleepless marathon.

Spots. Blurred vision. Brain not functioning correctly but you can't focus to identify what is off. Curb. Stop sign. Passing car. All in heightened animation you blink to buffer. Will you lose your mind, drugs administered intramuscularly in hospital white? Scared in that held breath horror heart stop way. Tired on a bone level while skin and superficial layers buzz a tangible vibration you try to match with physical gesture. Neck and wrists where arteries pulse. Unsettled sitz bones. Extremities peripheral a pulling in torso and survival. Spinning reel of thoughts like projector film that circles and flaps after the picture is done and light blasts the screen. Harness the circles and pull them into lines dragged across the page. Spin like a hoola hoop contest participant who doesn't want the ribbon doesn't want to keep spinning but has to. Can't stop. You can't crawl into bed with the dirty sheets that haven't been washed for 3 weeks. Close your eyes and ward off nauseusness. Stomach quease from speed. You want someone to grab you midsentence and squeeze you in an embrace to release the pressure building in the top of your head. Demand an intermission. *You are making these thoughts but could stop at any time.* Call for help get lost in the maze of switchboard with an answering machine at the end. You are just so tired. Apologize as if it is your fault.

Join the world of 24/7 laundromats and grocery stores. Mingle with nocturnal red eyed beings. Walk Stadium Avenue at 3 am. Dull streetlights some kind of green initiative. They don't light up shit. Fidget look over both shoulders feel underdressed. You want a sweater maybe a cap incognito in wee hour status. Enter Kroger because the fluorescent lights calm you. Neatly stacked rows of kleenex. Ice cream tubs in freezer section. Fresh bread technically day old past midnight. Watch the sun's absence, feel it on the other side of the planet making way towards you like turning to try to see your back in the mirror. Gravitate to the empty aisles. Yellow triscuit boxes, texture of plastic chip bags, glint of glass sauce bottles. You don't know what to get. Why you entered the store in the first place. Why the spaces are getting smaller and the 20 somethings yelling from aisle 9 *she wanted sour cream and onion not ranch* cause you to sweat. You need to leave the store. But the night, the walk home, your bed, your inability to sleep, your inability to breathe. Body panting. Clenched hands. *Loose as a goose* try to relax. Eyes blur. Shut. You slowly realize the guttural sobs are coming from you. Stray thread pulls. Unravels. Hem undone. Don't know. How to. Make it. Stop. There isn't room for everything in your body.

In 1873 an ambitious but ill-advised project was put through in an effort to connect Crystal Lake and Lake Michigan with a navigable channel. The original level of Crystal Lake was, at that time, much higher than its present level. The project was a complete failure in respect to its accomplishing its proposed purpose. The result was the lowering of the lake and exposing a wide stretch of beach around the entire lake and making possible the development of Crystal Lake as a resort and residential area as well as the site of the village of Beulah. This monument, erected by the people of Benzie county, stands at the original level of Crystal Lake.

from *The Tragedy of Crystal Lake* by Leonard L. Case

LAKE ETYMOLOGY

Before this outline shifted these trees were water. The bank covered in lake. Bluff submerged. A girl finds a shell in the back woods. Later she will find a stone with the smooth feel of waves. They misgauged depth. The lake responded. To connect one body of water to another. A risk of liquid proportions. Thin land strip providing container, disrupted. The vision of boat passage, increased navigational possibility and the limitless notion that blue should enter blue. Simple measurements and the girl would be underwater where now are woods and green. Her house would be fishes and rippled sand. At night she dreams gills. This is under. Under dream. Under where breath is held.

Archibald Jones, a fruit grower from Illinois, initiated the Betsie River Improvement Company with the mission to connect Lake Michigan with Crystal Lake. The Betsie River, which would link them, was wide enough for a small sized steam craft. There was no engineer consulted. Water poured through the channel overflowing the river banks. Crystal Lake lowered. Enter beach property. **Resorts from logging towns.** Frankfort. Beulah. Elberta. Benzonia. Enter boats carrying passengers for luxury weekends from Chicago, St. Louis, Milwaukee. Enter the Assembly on Crystal's South Shore. The round-the-lake race. Robinson Resort. Cold Brook Springs Park Trust. Add sailboats with brightly colored spinnakers. Place my mother and father at a party in Chicago. Skip the part where she refuses the date and sets him up with a friend. Focus on the cottage he owns in Frankfort. Skip to newlywed weekends they drive six hours from city sweat to the bluff overlooking Crystal Lake.

I was born a hundred years after the tragedy of Crystal Lake. Our cottage was built on land once lake bottom. Houses built and passed through generations because of Archibald Jones' mistake. The logging and cherries that sustained the area replaced by this body of water 8 miles wide, 2 miles across. Life gathers at the edge. Water at the center. Gives. Takes. The soil mixed with sand. The land remembers its old undulation. Forest for beach. There was no room for us then.

They give me the name of the sister who died. *Stephanie*. I am gilled and finned. Water trial. They must breathe for me. I fight my way back to fluid. To darkness under amnio and womb. Because they have given me your name I must swim. I must breathe under water. I must see in the dark. Tiny palms crowded with both our lifelines fighting to survive. I must live amphibious. I am one of two. Water. Land. Land. Water.

Land. I grow up in a house overlooking water. Mother walks the edge of the lake daily. She distrusts the wind, the sun, the waves that might push you to her feet. She walks anyway. Waits for the dead to come ashore. *Missing.* She can not say dead for seven years so she doesn't say anything. Shore. Mother. Silent. They say my name but not yours. Wind teaches me to speak. To form words aspirant and oval. No one sees me crawl toward the edge where land meets water. I try to enter where you exited. Suspended time. Death and birth the same year. No one tells me if I look like you.

Water. She slides off the prow. Life vest strapped tight. She slips through orange. Sees blue and then darker. Hands block the light. There is wave rhythm, a song below. Undertow. A storm above disturbs bottom sediment. Stephanie breathes water. Corkscrew curls arc upward, a halo. The weight of her body unfamiliar and light. She forgot the swimming lessons. Instructions to kick her legs. Her fear of putting her face in the water.

Mother is far away at the surface where the sailboat tosses from gale force winds. One of the mainstays breaks and the mast swings from the stern. The steel boom almost hits Father in the head. He struggles with rudder and line. Control. The steady wind and clear skies at the start. Lake effect storm swept over the bluffs. No warning. No signs. He knew how to read the water. It told him nothing. He would argue with this nothing until the events blurred yellow. The color of the boat. The color of her hair.

They yelled our name with the full power of their lungs. While your lungs filled.
The wind took their words and flung them across the lake. Mother underwater now.
Where is my baby? While I kicked from inside. *Breathe.*

One of two, I would not drown. A seamless shift between air and water. A natural swimmer, I practiced holding my breath in the upstairs bathtub. So I could stay under longer. Mother clocked me on a stopwatch. Lungs pushed me to the surface spitting for air.

In dreams, I searched for you. Swam past the drop off where light no longer filters down. To see my face looking back. To give you the lines in your palms. Blue. Reach. Sometimes only your bones, fragile and fishlike. Water burial. Or your eyes, blue like mine, floating to the surface to recognize me.

I swam for years before they told me. Water mixed with skin and bone. I was seven years old. *Missing* turned to *dead*. There was a death certificate with your name on the first line: my name.

I search for you under glass calm. Beach glass and driftwood, your heart buried in this lake. I find you singing a lullaby. Words you can't teach me. I come back to land without you.

I never leave this lake. Attend college in Traverse City. Become a grief counselor to work with words unspoken in my house. The drowned. The drowning. I try to give families of the deceased air to breath. Water gives. Water takes. A wave smashed over the breakwater pier in Frankfort throwing two boys into Lake Michigan. One lived. One died. *I am one of two.*

The wind blows out of the northeast, the direction the storm came from. We sing together between white caps. One hundred years before I was born and before you died, a man had the idea to connect one body of water to another.

ENTER AMNESIAC

                      silence   here
                      rust thick
                      oblong & swivel
                      this oxygen ship

                                            the only out
                                            the way you came

it depends on where you stand:

bird skeleton observatory

love letter with skylights

invitation door to jelly sound
carnival ride infinity curves

                                            ingredients of circles
                                            in exact proportions
                                                    stretch speed
                                                & clunk nothing
                                                    red to disturb
                                            what waits in wings

walk inside the vertebrae
this might be your funicular vision
a dot on an aerial photo
breathing horizontal
tracks retrograde

digest the stroke

hum

a suggestion
or a vein collapsed
excuse me
finger latch jumble
of nightmare flings

unwind black verticals

opportunity for reverse walking:

tilted plane

collapsible lungs

yield intimate

conversation

noted

take what you said back
inside I shut my blinds
oblong sensation
of arrows retracting

shoes   purse

dream
you
whatchamacallit
thief

Decide by how you walk through and where to stop. There are shadows, lines bending, sound, track lights on a balcony. Silence erected as different positions of the lips and tongue. Lose the step and try not to touch rust. The only out the way you came. Spiral signifies infinity. Torque a non-linear forever like a heart arrhythmia. The color of mud striated. Weathered steel. An indicator. A body. Which way do you wind, clockwise or counter? Change the breath tempo of these walls. Hold.

Stable meter closed then open until the end is a finish. The space merely a suggestion. Tictoc. Insert voices in a discourse of your choosing. Whirlpool eddy or vein collapsed. I write from the center where there is more volume than the narrow *excuse me* walkway to a latch-like finger tracing a journey longer than expected with the destination a dream jumble of nightmare and flying.

Egg cracked. Opening or ceiling. It depends on where you stand. Mechanics like the back of a wristwatch for this spinning. Incubator with a panel for chance, delinquent pink sweater, observer, unlocked umbrella, museum guard. The ellipse wants to be watched. An invitation door to its jelly bop jazz sound and carnival ride gratis curves. Slim then fat yet fragile bird skeleton observatory: love letters with sky.

Outside: Horizon. I feel separate like a dot on an aerial photo in blue and green. This might be your funicular vision. Inside: Becomes home by my breathing. Two way digestion. Horizontal track lines. Hold on to your feet. Shuttle forward and reverse (digest the stroke). Walk inside the vertebrae.

The trajectory spits me out black vertical drizzle on amphibious rock. Take the prior torque and flip it. What seams time? Subject thread, emotional response, calendar, *skinny years*, map, decision. The transit still and tacit. Are you outside?

Enter amnesiac like remembering birth. The walls scratch at light. A tilted plane collapses and tries to make up for failure. I listen for the louder shape. Misrepresent the surroundings. Collaborate steel with bodies thinking. Resist the pressure to hurry up and practice reverse walking.

Retract the gesture right angle and burnt sienna. No one walks over the border. Start from scratch and make it new like the woman with matching shoes and purse. Practice scare tactics with young children. I tuck myself into this oblong whatchamacallit with points like disclaimer arrows. Do you worry about a blind spot? Do you chance the effects? Shut your eyes and feel the shapes singing. A hinge or repetition to stay in the same place. Steel myself. Steal time. Blind spot thief.

QUIET ANATOMY

86

she was light on the bay rippled stories (untold) line the marrow
her bones solid shadows movement never betrayed (soft)
underside welcome inward gaze a strength she did not lie down
on the shore dream of memory (salt) (blood) figure foreground
against the sky body constellation discovered full bloom

archaeology

spaces inside her quiet still at rest on a lap give limb crease knee
hollow support of a neck (remember) there was wind sand dune
held grass stain backs her reflection skyward (you'd sing)
connect the light find north turn to face (yourself) hand mouth
(remember) cool lake air waded moonlit over rocks (you'd sing)
waves from the soles of her feet undertow (remember) long ride
home keep to (yourself) the road's middle line (you'd sing) radio
turned off the exit ramp go north (remember) we drove the night

ephemeral

She didn't want to admit. This love of other. Like herself.
(Superstitious.) She didn't go to homecoming. This was.
Cabernet Shiraz in August. Her mother found. The breadcrumbs
before the birds. She clenched her teeth (at night.) Only spoke
parts of words. Told a piece of paper. Then a friend.
Not a mirror. She believed reflections were only in people.
She wanted someone who looked like her. To think themselves
beautiful. *If a=b and b=c then a=c.* Her hands
were her voice when they shook. (Often.) She was alone.

periphery

she knocked on doors (patient) waiting rooms for an entrance
never to open her mouth to simple words: *hello / night / i love
you / burn* shame swallowed whiskey shots better to hold hands
underneath tables unseen the credits roll over in bed she slept
always the right side

circumspect

time was not a line she travelled well turning back on herself
(circles) knees rotation of head one foot after daredevil run
forward eyes closed distant arms *please catch* fall softened limbs
roll the ground pinned earth she did (not) get up

relinquish

(still) lives sketched before she left the (familiar) doors with
handles pushed down a corridor (empty) she could not find
moss on the trees the star (besides the sun) her obsession for
the horizon gave her a papercut when she got too close

labyrinth

she measured hours of sleep the amount of food she ate (silence)
like a wound vulnerable places did not speak (wrists)
(back of throat) where night was wind filled a hollow between
her (collarbones) she never explained the exits planned her

dysteleology

long silences satisfied her hair in face (insulation) from another
day she walked the weather front the tip of her heels imagined
rain-soaked hair in Florida light blouse (60's) in Houston
hibernation snowed in Cheyenne (her body) an atlas plotted
coordinates street corners intersections past present (always)
future always the curb guardrail off road open arms tailwinds
in her favor

latitude

she knew how to build a fire: hair ash turpentine coffee (ground)
cinder thoughts snapped awake from light *sleep well my love*
written on the inside of (used) books shopping list left in a
(library) book: *ketchup jam Campbell's soup rutabaga parsnips
toothpaste film* (candid) replies to a question posed body of
work a dedication to words they did not hurt her: *amsterdam /
port de bras / two / one*

vagabond

light in the (empty) room across the courtyard dusted snow cold sensation (absence a switch) darkness she could not hold in her mouth aftertaste gesture palm directed outward fairytale (circle) protection

condole

she was not interested in abridged days (elusive) thoughts
defined alphabetically her (second) language the body a
text unabridged travels annotated gesture forehead against
(cool) tile of shower her mourning a surprise amidst cello
vibrato and the smell of footsteps in snow

attuned

she walked away from the sun when it set her eyes on bright
colors red (blue) held in the iris gently mix (blue) red *purple* her
favorite: *eggplant / grapes / plums* skin her lips color tastes
(cool) evening air the birds (v formation) her body held breath
closed the day faded blank pages at the end of a novel

inversion

She hated acronyms. Words initialized by lack. Of time.
S(pace.) Beautiful words: *postscript / etcetera / repondez si
vous plait.* The names of states weekdays months: *minnesota /
wednesday / february.* Sound of letters unfolding: *as soon as
possible / university / regarding.* She read. The shadows
pronounced. Lists of emancipated. (Words.) Language was.
A river she did not wish to shorten. She spoke. Sentences aware.
How they took silences. (Breath.) The next. Word inside her.
(Body.)

atlas

sleep in december bookend of year wrapped with cellophane
her heart preserved in a library card catalog out of date contents
labeled *do not touch* she believed in lockboxes for valuables
her freedom to walk (alone)

recalcitrance

she was the she of every chromosome x or was it why does she
have to explain the in place of words fill the blanks *girl / woman*
broaden perspective she *she* less conceptual the she is me you
(anybody) a quicksand pulled from inside

empirical

CODA

Open Loop Triptych

(the understudy waits for cough or stumble in the wings an exchange of pronouns mops up the unsaid she takes keys out of hidden pockets and cradles grief so I can go to school and pretend stillness of hands she is the dancer lights off naked in a studio laughing because I is a slippery vessel that only holds spine and limbs a coat rack of costume what will I wear today on the other side a trapdoor with hinges that give unexpectedly I wait for the one I love only mystery shades her already familiar face after years of hiding the task of rerouting despair to the ocean a sunbather she reaches upward while I find endpoints to touch what is not my face exhausted expression of relief when the tide and all this water her doing and I keep silent in arid climates because sight saddens this detached version fastens itself around neck a slim snap to sacrifice a part for this steady persistence her beauty marked a flaw of division she could carry the spring I buried myself and take away the sin of what has left the eyes a carriage a drawn exit the joke she remembered when I forgot how to say yes fastened a framework to swing from without danger of noose and where I fail she continues relentless as morning)

(she yes she again in silence a misaligned comfort to match snow in October and the leaves turn away her frame slighter less sturdy from uphill travel slip of step when locomotion from one corner to the other was a way to speak she writes an entrance she does not enter barren I enter and she does not know to write an exit unlit a tunnel when supposed light and gentle acceleration instead clash and bump and nothing reflects the sullen her mother would say ghost and how could as she walked without sound unseen because too much entered the eye a retina detached and she pulled inward to live below her means the trail to follow entrance served exit when no other way presented I found her on the kitchen floor we rose in territories no one should go past the unbreakable kept safe like a doll eyes open and close when tilted when gravity is most kind)

(and she knew how to place hands on another and tilt her head in comfort but still this jangle of disbelief the date approaches and supposedly absent yet I am and continue to wear seatbelts when speed is unavoidable seven times a day ingestion to remember the ribbon laced around finger wife to capitulation the shiny wrappers line her bag this unloading channel blocker part of an experiment she leaned to see the steadiness of tides and it was easy one foot then a clear bridge with forced contraception her genes what would she leave as a marker to say here and here and especially there the going eventually to take leave and arrival desirable rather she wore the baseboards down foundation obstacle for flight)

She Had Windows for Organs

I picture her in that white dress pale as her skin arms extended in a horizon, something infinite. But it was her ears that brought people down the dirt road past the crossroads to her two-room cottage on the bank of the only water running through the mountain town. She knew how to listen. People told her things marrow and forgotten. She conversed with silences when no one came. Kept a diary:

leaf falling   floorboard creak   my heart going bust   wristwatch

She navigated the path along the creek stepping over tree roots and keeping the sun on the left side of her face. She never got lost and never opened her eyes till she got to the meadow with the bench in the middle.

I spoke with her on that bench. She listened to me while surveying the flight pattern of geese over my right shoulder. When I was done, which took a bit, she stood up and said:

Tributary. You are all branches and won't make it to the ocean if you keep it up.

I know what she means now. Then I thought maybe what folks said about her being a bit off was true. But actually, she just perceived more than most and didn't bother making it sound regular if it wasn't. *Tributary.* I fought with that word until it led me fresh. Now I am saltwater and tide.

NOTES AND COMMENTARY

FIELD NOTES

Notes as gateway into the life and living that created the text. The book becomes a three dimensional body, these traces small invitations into the movements, memory and dreams, the life of the book as it breathes itself in your hands. Thank you for your entry. You are a vehicle moving the pages and giving the words alternate lives. The beauty of collaboration. Here is an offering of the specific geographies and bodymind states that incubated these pieces for me. Not as layer onto your own experience. Rather a field of traversal, a passing through. Notice what clings to your ankles changing your stride or brushes an image in an unexpected direction. An attempt to enrich the soil and make transparent the elements. Water always. These notes are a lubrication, to make fluid and mobile the contents.

As a poet and dancer, there is delight in the exchange between forms – movement to words, words to movement until the lines between disciplines become curves and then circles. Dance was my first language. Poetry was always woven into my creative practice but came into the foreground when movement wasn't available to me due to disability. To continue to move and do what I love, words offered another way to sculpt space in the choreography of a poem.

As a queer woman, desire between women runs through these pages as exploration of sexual aliveness and connections in various forms – lovers, sisters, city makers. The pronoun "she" provides background for a dictionary of invented entries, a parenthetical language of codes and a palette to write a coming into the body.

As a disabled person, someone living with bipolar disorder, there are the specific tracks my particular experiences with mental health difference leave on the work. I value these. Navigating my bodymind through shifting states is another artistic discipline. This discipline also defines and organizes my artistic trajectory. I work with changeable fluxes in energy, interest, concentration, capacities. Labile depression, mania, hypomania and mixed states. Periods when I'm not able to read or write.

These are some of the invisible tracks. I thought this book would be published posthumously. In a recent five year period of intense depression and suicidality, many hospitalizations and treatments including electroconvulsive therapy, I included an earlier version of *The Color She Gave Gravity* with my suicide note. I placed the manuscript in a manila folder with instructions to loved ones to try to find a publisher.

When I was ready to reread my old manuscript there were sections I didn't remember writing. The shock treatments caused brain damage and long term memory loss. I wasn't sure whether to enter into these poems or ditch the whole project for something new. I wasn't sure if I could still write. I wasn't sure how to bridge my shifted bodymind with the bodymind that had written these poems.

Movement and place provided a bridge. Much of the work had been written in specific somatic practices and/or locations.

"Penumbra" was created inside a structured movement improvisation. I invented a city to hold my dance partner, who was experiencing extreme mind states of psychosis, and my own life with bipolar disorder.

"Enter Amnesiac" was written inside Richard Serra's sculpture installation *The Matter of Time* at the Guggenheim Museum in Bilbao, Spain. I took on his quote, "I consider space to be a material" and worked with writing prose blocks while moving and sitting inside his massive steel structures in the grid of other museum goers. Later I carved these pieces playing with what remained and what fell away.

"Z Cycle" was made while I was experiencing mixed and manic states. It was the first piece I wrote after the hiatus. My idea was to begin writing slowly, but it was actually a flurry driven by this shift into mania highlighted by insomnia.

I initiated overhaul and revision through working with the manuscript in authentic movement. This practice involves following impulse and desire to move with eyes closed while being witnessed. I took lines of "Penumbra" and invited the words to take new shapes. I spoke a line and then moved, letting the language unfold. Then my partner offered a movement response based on her witnessing, and I jotted down a written response.

Crystal Lake in Northern Michigan is a landscape important to these traces. It is the engineering failure featured in "Lake Etymology." It is where I revise best, perhaps due to water's reminder of containment and flexibility. And it is where I'm now writing these notes at a desk with lake winds cooling my skin and blue out my peripheral vision with my beloved out in the deep swimming.

So these are traces. For me, this particular book is about survival, not in content, but in its existence in the world and my existence alongside it. More a thriving. I'm incredibly grateful to be here. I dedicate this to all the people who helped me stay. And for Petra who makes it beautiful.

Stephanie Heit
Frankfort, MI

THE COLOR OF VISIBLE
PHOTOGRAPHS BY GWYNNETH VANLAVEN

My interest in the topic of visibility comes from both my critique of visual culture and personal need. Since I was struck, pinned, and disabled by a car in 2007 while walking on the safety of a sidewalk, I have wondered how to keep others and myself safe from similar fates. I notice the fluorescent lime green vests that police and rescue workers wear, as well as construction workers, trash collectors, joggers and cyclists. The color has now taken hold as a fashion trend, from pantsuits to lace panties underneath.

I began research into the properties that make this color visible, and how it was chosen as the new standard warning signal for pedestrian safety. This touches on colorimetrics, semiotics, and human factors research. Curiously, we can imagine that our vibrant "visibility cloaks" might stop or slow an oncoming car and protect us from injury or death. In the desperate sales of all things colored visible, there comes the pressure of responsibility. For those whose activities involve crossings with cars, it is as if without the garb a pedestrian victim is reckless and culpable. Thus the burden to scream out, via hyper-visibility, our right to occupy space safely, becomes our own.

I wonder what happens as the trend continues. As the color pops up everywhere, will this diminish the awakening effect on motorists? How far can we amp up the volume on the visibility dial? At the core I wonder, who is visible? Does visibility make us safer or more vulnerable? Can everyone be equally visible? How do we keep a sense of safety in a world that feels chaotic and over-sped?

In my photographic series *The Color of Visible*, I center on this designated safety color fluorescent yellow-green. This color shrouds, cloaks, and envelops me. With light from automobile headlights, the gestures and textures bespeak both dwelling in and departure from the memory of being struck by a car. Performing through long exposures, I uncover new territory in relationship to color, safety, and memory.

My camera work explores motion and stillness in photography as in life. A camera is said to capture, or freeze an action in time and space. So too does a traumatic event. Unable to stop the car hurtling toward my place on the sidewalk, I feel captured by memory and frozen. I use photography to unfreeze, in order to create something new. The thaw nurtures spaces between dreaming and waking, between safety and vulnerability, and between self and other.

ACKNOWLEDGMENTS

Thank you to the editors and publishers of the following journals in which some of these poems have appeared: *Midwestern Gothic, Streetnotes, Nerve Lantern, Typo, Spoon Knife Anthology, For Immediate Release, Watching the Wheels: A Blackbird*. Gratitude to Nightboat Poetry Prize where this book was a finalist and to Ahsahta Press where an earlier version was a Sawtooth Poetry Prize finalist.

I want to celebrate the people and places that have informed and held my writing and movement throughout this book creation. From the beginning, Max Regan, extraordinary teacher and support. Forty Fingers Press: Claudia F. Savage, Joanna Preucel and Gabrielle Edison, for our continued poetry exchange and friendship. Barbara Dilley, for Contemplative Dance Practice in which some of this work was written. Naropa University Community where many of these pieces were seeded, heartfelt thanks to Anne Waldman, Bhanu Kapil, Eleni Sikelianos, Laird Hunt and Michelle Naka Pierce. Katharine Kaufman and Marija Krtolica for improvisational performance that led to the writing of a city. Michigan's Benzie County whose waters and landscape served as touchstone and respite for intensive revision and renewal. Christina Ryan-Stoltz, Jenn Ryan and all the women in the Benzie writing group. JoAnna Pepe. Sarah Michas-Martin for the prompt that led to Z Cycle. Julie Carr for insight and overhaul. Brooke Wear and Debra Horowitz, words fail. Hector Saldivia Campos, mil gracias. University of Michigan Initiative on Disability Studies and disability culture activists. Washtenaw County National Alliance on Mental Illness. Gwynneth VanLaven for her photography. Kundalini yoga community. Stefanie Cohen and the authentic movement group. Summer Rodman, Andrew Wille, Denise Leto, Sophia Galifianakis: writing allies. Lynne DeSilva-Johnson, book artist doula, for giving me and this work such a vibrant and caring home at The Operating System. My parents, Judy and Roger Heit. My partner in life and creativity, Petra Kuppers.

ABOUT THE AUTHOR

Stephanie Heit is a poet, dancer, and teacher of somatic writing, Contemplative Dance Practice, and Kundalini Yoga. She lives with bipolar disorder and is a member of the Olimpias, an international disability performance collective. She makes her home in Ann Arbor, Michigan with her partner and collaborator, Petra Kuppers.

WHY PRINT / DOCUMENT?

*The Operating System uses the language "print document" to differentiate from the book-object as part of our mission to distinguish the act of documentation-in-book-FORM from the act of publishing as a backwards facing replication of the book's agentive *role* as it may have appeared the last several centuries of its history. Ultimately, I approach the book as TECHNOLOGY: one of a variety of printed documents (in this case bound) that humans have invented and in turn used to archive and disseminate ideas, beliefs, stories, and other evidence of production.*

Ownership and use of printing presses and access to (or restriction of) printed materials has long been a site of struggle, related in many ways to revolutionary activity and the fight for civil rights and free speech all over the world. While (in many countries) the contemporary quotidian landscape has indeed drastically shifted in its access to platforms for sharing information and in the widespread ability to "publish" digitally, even with extremely limited resources, the importance of publication on physical media has not diminished. In fact, this may be the most critical time in recent history for activist groups, artists, and others to insist upon learning, establishing, and encouraging personal and community documentation practices. Hear me out.

With The OS's print endeavors I wanted to open up a conversation about this: the ultimately radical, transgressive act of creating PRINT /DOCUMENTATION in the digital age. It's a question of the archive, and of history: who gets to tell the story, and what evidence of our life, our behaviors, our experiences are we leaving behind? We can know little to nothing about the future into which we're leaving an unprecedentedly digital document trail — but we can be assured that publications, government agencies, museums, schools, and other institutional powers that be will continue to leave BOTH a digital and print version of their production for the official record. Will we?

As a (rogue) anthropologist and long time academic, I can easy pull up many accounts about how lives, behaviors, experiences — how THE STORY of a time or place — was pieced together using the deep study of correspondence, notebooks, and other physical documents which are no longer the norm in many lives and practices. As we move our creative behaviors towards digital note taking, and even audio and video, what can we predict about future technology that is in any way assuring that our stories will be accurately told – or told at all?

As a creative practitioner, the stories, journals, and working notes of other creative practitioners have been enormously important to me. And yet so many creative people of this era no longer put together physical documents of their work – no longer have physical archives of their writing or notebooks, typed from the first draft to the last, on computers. Even visual artists often no longer have non-digital slides and portfolios. How will we leave these things for the record?

How will we say WE WERE HERE, WE EXISTED, WE HAVE A DIFFERENT STORY?

/////////THE OPERATING SYSTEM IS A QUESTION, NOT AN ANSWER.

THIS is not a fixed entity.

The OS is an ongoing experiment in resilient creative practice which necessarily morphs as its conditions and collaborators change. It is not a magazine, a website, or a press, but rather an ongoing dialogue ABOUT the act of publishing on and offline: it is an exercise in the use and design of both of these things and their role in our shifting cultural landscape, explored THROUGH these things.

I see publication as documentation: an act of resistance, an essential community process, and a challenge to the official story / archive, and I founded the OS to exemplify my belief that people everywhere can train themselves to use self or community documentation as the lifeblood of a resilient, independent, successful creative practice.

The name "THE OPERATING SYSTEM" is meant to speak to an understanding of the self as a constantly evolving organism, which just like any other system needs to learn to adapt if it is to survive. Just like your computer, you need to be "updating your software" frequently, as your patterns and habits no longer serve you. Our intentions above all are empowerment and unsilencing, encouraging creators of all ages and colors and genders and backgrounds and disciplines to reclaim the rights to cultural storytelling, and in so doing to the historical record of our times and lives.

Bob Holman once told me I was "scene agnostic" and I took this as the highest compliment: indeed, I seek work and seek to make and promote work that will endure and transcend tastes and trends, making important and asserting value rather than being told was has and has not.

The OS has evolved in quite a short time from an idea to a growing force for change and possibility: in a span of 5 years, from 2013-2017, we will have published more than 40 volumes from a hugely diverse group of contributors, and solicited and curated thousands of pieces online, collaborating with artists, composers, choreographers, scientists, futurists, and so many more. Online, you'll also find partnerships with cultural organizations modelling the value of archival process documentation.

Beginning in 2016, our new series :: "Glossarium: Unsilenced Texts and Modern Translations", had as its first volume a dual language Arabic-English translation of Palestinian poet and artist Ashraf Fayadh's "Instructions Within," followed by three Cuban Spanish-English translations by Margaret Randall.

There is ample room here for you to expand and grow your practice ...and your possibility. Join us.

- Lynne DeSilva-Johnson, Founder/Managing Editor,
THE OPERATING SYSTEM, Brooklyn NY 2016

TITLES IN THE PRINT: DOCUMENT COLLECTION

An Absence So Great and Spontaneous It Is Evidence of Light - Anne Gorrick [2018]
Chlorosis - Michael Flatt and Derrick Mund [2018]
Death is a Festival - Anis Shivani [2018]
Return Trip / Viaje Al Regreso; Dual Language Edition - Israel Dominguez,(trans. Margaret Randall) [2018]
Born Again - Ivy Johnson [2018]
Singing for Nothing - Wally Swist [2018]
One More Revolution - Andrea Mazzariello [2017]
Fugue State Beach - Filip Marinovich [2017]
Lost City Hydrothermal Field - Peter Milne Greiner [2017]
The Book of Everyday Instruction - Chloe Bass [2017]
In Corpore Sano : Creative Practice and the Challenged Body [Anthology, 2017]
Lynne DeSilva-Johnson and Jay Besemer, co-editors
Love, Robot - Margaret Rhee[2017]
Nothing Is Wasted - Shabnam Piryaei [2017]
You Look Something - Jessica Tyner Mehta [2017]
CHAPBOOK SERIES 2017 : INCANTATIONS
featuring original cover art by Barbara Byers
sp. - Susan Charkes; Radio Poems - Jeffrey Cyphers Wright; Fixing a Witch/Hexing the Stitch - Jacklyn Janeksela;
cosmos a personal voyage by carl sagan ann druyan steven sotor and me - Connie Mae Oliver
Flower World Variations, Expanded Edition/Reissue - Jerome Rothenberg and Harold Cohen [2017]
Island - Tom Haviv [2017]
What the Werewolf Told Them / Lo Que Les Dijo El Licantropo - Chely Lima (trans. Margaret Randall) [2017]
The Color She Gave Gravity - Stephanie Heit [2017]
The Science of Things Familiar - Johnny Damm[Graphic/Poetry Hybrid, 2017]
agon - Judith Goldman [2017]
To Have Been There Then / Estar Alli Entonces - Gregory Randall (trans. Margaret Randall) [2017]

Instructions Within - Ashraf Fayadh [2016]
Arabic-English dual language edition; Mona Kareem, translator
Let it Die Hungry - Caits Meissner [2016]
A GUN SHOW - Adam Sliwinski and Lynne DeSilva-Johnson;
So Percussion in Performance with Ain Gordon and Emily Johnson [2016]
Everybody's Automat [2016] - Mark Gurarie
How to Survive the Coming Collapse of Civilization [2016] - Sparrow
CHAPBOOK SERIES 2016: OF SOUND MIND
featuring the quilt drawings of Daphne Taylor
Improper Maps - Alex Crowley; While Listening - Alaina Ferris;
Chords - Peter Longofono; Any Seam or Needlework - Stanford Cheung
TEN FOUR - Poems, Translations, Variations [2015]- Jerome Rothenberg, Ariel Resnikoff, Mikhl Likht
MARILYN [2015] - Amanda Ngoho Reavey
CHAPBOOK SERIES 2015: OF SYSTEMS OF
featuring original cover art by Emma Steinkraus
Cyclorama - Davy Knittle; The Sensitive Boy Slumber Party Manifesto - Joseph Cuillier;
Neptune Court - Anton Yakovlev; Schema - Anurak Saelow
SAY/MIRROR [2015; 2nd edition 2016] - JP HOWARD
Moons Of Jupiter/Tales From The Schminke Tub [plays, 2014] - Steve Danziger
CHAPBOOK SERIES 2014: BY HAND
Pull, A Ballad - Maryam Parhizkar; Executive Producer Chris Carter - Peter Milne Grenier;
Spooky Action at a Distance - Gregory Crosby; Can You See that Sound - Jeff Musillo
CHAPBOOK SERIES 2013: WOODBLOCK
featuring original prints from Kevin William Reed
Strange Coherence - Bill Considine;; The Sword of Things - Tony Hoffman;
Talk About Man Proof - Lancelot Runge / John Kropa;
An Admission as a Warning Against the Value of Our Conclusions -Alexis Quinlan

DOC U MENT
/däkyə mə nt/

First meant "instruction" or "evidence," whether written or not.

noun - a piece of written, printed, or electronic matter that provides information or evidence or that serves as an official record
verb - record (something) in written, photographic, or other form
synonyms - paper - deed - record - writing - act - instrument

[*Middle English, precept, from Old French, from Latin documentum, example, proof, from docre, to teach; see dek- in Indo-European roots.*]

Who is responsible for the manufacture of value?

Based on what supercilious ontology have we landed in a space where we vie against other creative people in vain pursuit of the fleeting credibilities of the scarcity economy, rather than freely collaborating and sharing openly with each other in ecstatic celebration of MAKING?

While we understand and acknowledge the economic pressures and fear-mongering that threatens to dominate and crush the creative impulse, we also believe that **now more than ever we have the tools to relinquish agency via cooperative means,** fueled by the fires of the Open Source Movement.

Looking out across the invisible vistas of that rhizomatic parallel country
we can begin to see our community beyond constraints,
in the place where intention meets resilient, proactive, collaborative organization.

Here is a document born of that belief, sown purely of imagination and will.
When we document we assert. We print to make real, to reify our being there.
When we do so with mindful intention to address our process,
to open our work to others, to create beauty in words in space, to respect and acknowledge the strength of the page we now hold physical, a thing in our hand...
we remind ourselves that, like Dorothy: *we had the power all along, my dears.*

THE PRINT! DOCUMENT SERIES

is a project of
the trouble with bartleby
in collaboration with
the operating system

www.ingramcontent.com/pod-product-compliance
Lightning Source LLC
Chambersburg PA
CBHW081337080526
44588CB00017B/2649